33 KIDS MONOLOGUES

By Alex Swenson

A Collection of Monologues

For Children

Ages 4-13 Years Old

TABLE OF CONTENTS

MONOLOGUES FOR KIDS AGES 7-10 YEARS OLD

GIRL

Comedic Monologues

Dramatic Monologues

BOY

Comedic Monologues

Dramatic Monologues

MONOLOGUES FOR KIDS AGES 11-13 YEARS OLD

GIRL

Comedic Monologues

Dramatic Monologues

BOY

Comedic Monologues

Dramatic Monologues

To Mark, Nikita and Diego, who inspire me every day.

FOREWORD

Thank you for purchasing this collection of kids monologues.

For ease of use, the monologues are organized into 3 categories according to age range:

- Monologues for kids 4 – 6 years old
- Monologues for kids 7 – 10 years old
- Monologues for kids 11 - 13 years old

These categories refer to the *age range* of the characters, not the actual age of your child, so help kids pick a monologue that reflect the roles they would audition for.

Of course, every child is different, so pick something that is not "too old" for a young actor's maturity level and most importantly, something they relate to and find FUN!

Monologues for 4-6 year olds are divided only between boy, girl, and boy or girl monologues.

All the other monologues are divided into two categories for boys and girls: dramatic and comedic.

Many of the monologues in this book can be used for a boy or a girl, so I encourage you to read everything within one age range. This way, you won't skip a piece that would be perfect for your child.

Every monologue in this book is under a minute and a half, which is all you need for an audition or competition. You'll find that the monologues for very young children are slightly shorter while the tween monologues are slightly longer.

I hope these monologues help your kids nail acting auditions and reach their dreams. We love to get feedback, so please share your success stories with these monologues by contacting us at www.acting-school-stop.com/contact-us.html.

Also feel free to contact us to inquire about any reproduction rights. You are free to print the monologues for your personal use and to perform them at auditions, but all other rights are reserved, including reproducing any part of this book by electronic means.

For more information, visit our website at www.acting-school-stop.com. It contains a section for parents of child actors where you will find informational articles on how to pick the right child acting class, find an agent for your child, help them nail acting auditions, and more.

I hope you enjoy the book and most importantly, that your kids have FUN performing the monologues!

Alex Swenson

MONOLOGUES FOR KIDS
AGES 4-6 YEARS OLD

Girl Monologue

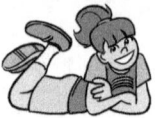

No Goblins Allowed

Samantha talks about the special secret place in her house and the goblin who keeps trying to break in.

SAMANTHA:

I have a special little place in my house. It's under the stairs. My mom put some stars on the ceiling that shine in the dark. I put pictures of fairies on the walls. I have a special pillow and blanket in my special place, and magical books.

I'm the only one who can go there. No monsters are allowed. No witches, no trolls, no crocodiles and no spiders. They all know the rule… Except the goblin. He keeps trying to come in. He bangs on the door and breaks everything with his baby spoon. He's 2 years old. My parents say he's my little brother but I know better. He walks funny, just like a goblin. And he talks all the time but no one understands.

I wish he could understand this: "NO GOBLINS ALLOWED!"

Girl Monologue

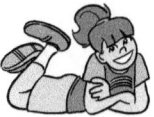

How to Be a Princess

Isabella shares with the audience how to be a princess, how to find a prince and marry your daddy.

ISABELLA:

Hello, my name is Isabella and I am a princess. I was born once upon a time in a land far far away. I have an evil stepmother who is a queen and makes me work hard cleaning the house. But that's OK because I have a beautiful dress, I don't eat any poisoned apples, and I never prick my finger on a spinning wheel.

The nice thing about being a princess is I know how to find a prince. If you want I can show you. It's very easy. You just close your eyes and look like you're dead like this and a prince will come to kiss you. You can try it, but you have to put on your princess dress first or he won't know you're a princess and he won't kiss you. But you'll know he's a prince, even if he's been changed into a beast by a bad witch, because of the kiss of true love.

My daddy's a prince. I think I'll marry him some day. But first I have to sleep for 100 years. That should make me old enough.

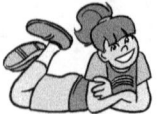

Girl Monologue

The Tooth Fairy With a Mission

Eva has just been told some bad news by her dentist about the tooth fairy.

EVA:

I just heard some bad news. The tooth fairy wants to fight cavities and now she's tough. She only takes your teeth and gives you a gift if you brushed them every day. If your tooth is all dirty, she'll just leave it and you don't get anything except cavities. If you've been eating a lot of candy and not brushing your teeth, it's even more trouble. The tooth fairy will come at night and take your teddy bear. That's what the teeth doctor said.

But don't worry, it's not true. My mom told me, it's just *stare tactics*. Good kids who brush their teeth don't have anything to worry about really. My mom says the tooth fairy has to "meet her quota".

I don't know what that means but it sounds like we'll be OK.

Boy Monologue

When I Grow Up

Richard complains to his Mommy about a day at pre-K when all the kids got to draw a picture of what they wanted to be when they grew up, except him.

RICHARD:

It's not fair. The teacher said, "What do you want to be when you grow up?" My friend Kyle said, "A fireman" and he got to draw a nice fire truck and fire station with his name on it. Jackson said, "A policeman". He got some cool shiny black and white paper to make a police car. Kaitlin said, "A princess", and she got some glitter glue to make a dress. I'm the only one who didn't get to be what I wanted. There's even a kid who wanted to be a fireman-policeman-Spiderman, and he got some cotton to make a spider web! But I said I wanted to be a conductor and the teacher made me draw the picture of a train.

(beat)

You think she doesn't like music, mommy?

Boy Monologue

Birthday Tantrum

Elliot had so much fun at his birthday party, he doesn't want to go to bed. He decides to give a tantrum a try.

ELLIOT:

I don't want to go to bed! I'm a big kid. I'm not a baby anymore. I had my birthday party so now I'm old. I want to stay here and play with my presents. I don't want to ever sleep again. Sleeping is for babies. Parents don't sleep. I hear you after you put me to bed. You're not sleeping! Parents play all night. I want to play! I want to eat M&Ms and birthday cake again. I want to jump in the birthday house. I want another birthday party right NOW! I want to be big!

(beat)

Mommy, I'm tired, can you carry me to bed?

Boy Monologue

First Day of School

Charley is starting kindergarten tomorrow, but he wonders if he wouldn't be better off not growing up so fast.

CHARLEY:

It's my first day at school tomorrow. I really want to go, but I feel sick. I don't want to be sick but what can I do? Listen, I'm coughing.

(Charley fakes a cough.)

My friend Carlos went to school last year. He never came back. I don't know what happened to him. My uncle Tommy told me kindergarten teachers make kids sit all day without moving and if they move they tie them to the chair. He's silly. Teachers are nice... Right?

My dad says I'm going to become a man at school. But he doesn't have to go to school. He sounds really happy. I don't feel really happy. My tummy hurts. Is it really that important to become a man? My dad is a man. He works all the time. He never plays with me.

I think I'd like to stay a kid this year. Maybe I can be a man next year.

Boy or Girl Monologue

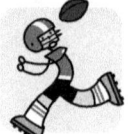

The Firefighter Trick

Jordan talks about a fire drill at his school and how he learned about things that are dangerous.

JORDAN:

Mr. Fire came to our school yesterday. He's the one who drives the fire truck and fights the fire. He came to show us a fire drill. He said if you see a fire you have to run away really fast. And all my friends ran really fast outside to the playground.

But I told Mr. Fire, I'm not moving, because I'm very courageous, and I can make myself very strong and very tall and say in a really scary voice, "Go away, fire!" and the fire is going to be so scared of me. Mr. Fire said it was better not to be courageous, because a fire is just too dangerous.

Today I have to get my shots. I think it's better not to be courageous and just run away. I'm going to tell the doctor, "It's just too dangerous!"

Boy or Girl Monologue

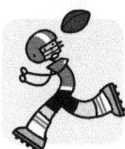

The Divorce

Pat has a classmate whose parents are getting a divorce. He talks to his dad, who is going away on a business trip, about his fears of the same thing happening to him.

PAT:

I don't want you to go on a business trip, Dad.

Sara Furtiz at school said her dad went on a business trip, and then he was gone a long time, and then he came back but just to say hello, and now he doesn't stay at her house anymore. She has to go see him in another house and she has another room over there. She had to split up all her toys and all her teddy bears. She can only take Miss Billy with her because that's her favorite teddy, but all her other things have to stay in her house.

Sara Furtiz says her dad was going to a divorce on his business trip. She said her dad was sad because he had to go to the divorce all by himself, and that's when everything happened.

Dad, if you go to a divorce, can I come with you?

Boy or Girl Monologue

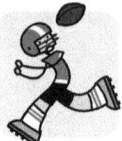

Too Many Questions

Eva is asking her mom a lot of questions, and sometimes even Mom doesn't have an answer, especially when it comes to how to make babies.

EVA:

Mom, why is it raining today? But why is the sun not here? Where does the rain come from? Are the clouds angry? Where do the clouds go when they're done? Mom, what's behind the sky? And what's behind the universe?

(Mom has no answer for this one. Eva digs into her breakfast bowl. Beat.)

Mom, why do cheerios have a hole in it? Is it for the milk to get through? Why do I like Cheerios but my friend Johnny doesn't? Because we're different? Are my friends the twins different? Why do they look the same?

They come from the same seed?! I didn't know babies grew from seeds. Can we plant some in our garden?

(beat)

If we can't plant babies, how do you make them?

(Mom doesn't have an answer.)

It's OK if you don't know, Mommy.

MONOLOGUES FOR KIDS AGES 7-10 YEARS OLD

Girl Monologue - Comedic

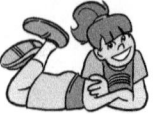

Girl's Fib

Kate is not very good at telling the truth, but she's pretty good at making up stories to get out of trouble when she does something bad, like ruining her mother's new dress.

KATE:

I swear, Mom, it wasn't me who cut up your nice red dress. I don't know how it got in my room. I saw the cat running around your closet. Maybe... it fell down from the hanger on her head and then she couldn't see and she got scared and dragged it all the way into my bedroom.

I was just reading my book. I didn't see anything. Then I went out to have a snack, and... Oh, that's probably when the mean Barbie came in! She loves to steal pretty dresses. I've had a few problems with her before. She probably saw your dress and decided to cut it all up to see if it could fit her. Yes, I'm sure that's what happened. I'm sure my good Barbie saw the whole thing. Let me go ask her.

(beat)

Yes, that's it! The mean Barbie did it. But don't worry, I took care of it. I put her on the thinking chair and said, "Little lady, you're not moving until you apologize."

Girl Monologue - Comedic

Ask Me to Be your Girlfriend

Savannah, a little girl with a little attitude, asks her best friend if he wants to be her boyfriend, but knows how to save face when she doesn't get the answer she wants.

SAVANNAH:

Hey, would you like to be boyfriend and girlfriend?

(beat)

What do you mean I can't ask? Because I'm a girl? When were you born? The twentieth century?

Fine, you ask me then. Ask me what? Ask me if I want to be your girlfriend, dummy! Or don't ask me, see if I care. I've got plenty of boys who would love for me to be their girlfriend so I'm not going to be waiting for you!

I know you haven't asked me! But I'm just saying, if you did ask me I would say no. First of all, you don't know how to blow bubbles with your gum. Who doesn't know how to blow *Bubble* Gum? Second, your mom puts iron-ons on the back pocket of your jeans. That's nerdy. And last but not least, you like Fruit Loops and I like Corn Pops. If we don't even like the same breakfast cereal, how can we be married some day?

Well, I don't want to marry you either, so stop asking me to be your girlfriend!

Girl Monologue - Comedic

The Overscheduled kid

Between soccer, ballet and swim team, Kaitlin just doesn't have time for her mom anymore, unless she can convince her to help...

KAITLIN:

I'm sorry Mom, but I don't have time to do stuff together anymore. If you want to hang out, you're going to have to make an appointment. Ok, let me get my schedule.

(beat)

Well, as you know, a kid's gotta go to school, so weekdays are out until 3 pm. Monday I have soccer practice. Tuesday is swim team. I can't miss swimming. We're preparing for the intercity competition. And then Wednesday the math tutor is coming. You called him. Remember how I got an A minus last week and you freaked out? I told you it wasn't a big deal but you didn't want me to fall behind in school.

And then you heard all the parents at the PTO meeting talking about how well my friend Sara plays the piano and you signed me up for music lessons. That's on Thursday. But we can cancel... Of course I want "a musical ear"! Yes, Mom, piano sounds *really* fun. Well, Friday is my last rehearsal for the ballet recital on Saturday, so all that's left after handball in the morning is Sunday afternoon for studying.

But don't worry, I have an idea. If you do my homework all week, I can book you for all Sunday afternoon!

Girl Monologue - Dramatic

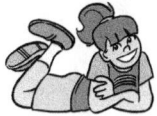

An Essay from the Heart

Maria is reading an essay she wrote about an event that changed her life in front of her class.

MARIA:

"Describe an event that changed your life."

If I had to describe an event that changed my life, I would have to say that it was the day I found Frizz. I don't really know how he fell into our backyard but I loved him right away. My dad said he was a newborn kitten and someone threw him over the wall to get rid of him. He was like a tiny ball of fur so I called him Frizz.

He was hungry, but he was too little to drink milk like other cats, so I took a syringe from my doctor play kit and gave him some milk that way. But he couldn't drink very well. He was too scared. I told him it would be all right. I put him on the inside of my arm and he calmed down because he could hear the heart beat in my wrist and it made him feel safe. Maybe he thought I was his mommy.

He closed his eyes and I watched him sleep. And then he stopped breathing. And he got cold. My mom said it was too much of a fall for him, but I think he died of sadness because he felt all alone in the world. I wish he could have seen inside my heart. I wanted to tell him I loved him, but I didn't speak cat.

Girl Monologue - Dramatic

It's OK to Say Sorry

Ella hasn't heard from her dad since he left 6 months ago. After a fight with her mom, she decides to write him a letter. In this monologue, she is reading her letter aloud to herself to make sure she likes it.

ELLA:

Dear Dad,

I've never written a letter to you before because I was angry. I thought you didn't love me and that's why you left and never visit. But now I understand everything, and I want to tell you that it's OK.

Mom said you had to leave because you did something bad. I did something bad too. I got a C on my test and I didn't want Mom to know so I turned it into a B. But she found out anyway. When I saw how mad she was, I really didn't want to say the truth, so I got more mad and ran to my room. Now I feel sad. Everybody is eating apple pie downstairs and I'm stuck here, starving!

Is that how you feel, Dad? Like everybody's eating apple pie without you? Well, I just wanted you to know that whatever is the bad thing you did, whether it was lying about your grades or worse, it's OK. You can say sorry and we'll forgive you. I think it's better to say sorry than to miss out on all the fun, don't you? OK, I'm going to try it now. If you get this in the mail, then it worked and you can do it too.

I'll be waiting for you. Love, Ella

Girl Monologue - Dramatic

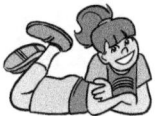

A Lesson for the Dolls

Cora's dad has been hitting her. In this monologue, she teaches her dolls how to stay out of trouble.

CORA:

OK, dolls, here are the rules if we don't want to get hit.

Rule 1: No dolls on the floor. You know how Dad gets if he's in a bad mood when he gets home and you guys are all over the floor, right? I'm not asking you to clean my room, but get out of the way when you hear the door slam, OK?

Rule 2: Don't let my sister play with you. If we get into a fight because of you and end up making a ruckus, you know what will happen, so help out please and don't let anything get started.

Rule 3: Learn the signs. When Dad doesn't say much when he comes home from work, that's when he had a bad day. Do what I do. Make yourself scarce and very quiet. Try to stay in your room if you can but don't be late to dinner, and make sure your hands and fingernails are extra clean.

Dolls? If the rules don't work, can you please come and help? Mommy's too scared and I can't tell anyone else about this. You're my only friends. I'll look after you. I'll keep you forever when I grow up and take you far far away from here. But please help me, please.

Boy Monologue - Comedic

The Big News

Kyle tells his friend about the big news he just got from his parents.

KYLE:

Ok, so my mom and dad come in my room and say they have a big surprise for me. I thought for sure it was the new Batmobile we saw at Target. I know it's not my birthday or anything but it's really cool so I followed all the rules when I saw it. I didn't whine. I just said, "Wow, what a cool Batmobile." I even used my cute voice to tell my mom, "See, I'm not asking for it." So I was sure that was the surprise.

Well, guess what the surprise was? *Your mom is having a baby.*

I thought kids like me were out of danger after 2nd grade. "Isn't Mom too old to have a baby?" I said. Mom said she didn't like my question. I said I didn't like her surprise. At this point, it wasn't looking good at all for the Batmobile, so I thought I may as well ask the *really scary* question: "Is it a girl?"

Yes! A girl!

I am going to have to share my room, my toys, my parents, my life with a GIRL. Yuk! I said, "I don't want a little sister" and... well, I was crying. And then the most amazing thing happened. My parents gave me the Batmobile.

I think this baby thing may turn out good for me.

Boy Monologue - Comedic

The Black Pirate

Jack, a boy with a big imagination, is playing pirate with his friend, but having a hard time sharing.

JACK:

All right, I'm the black pirate and you're the white pirate. You take the guns... What? Your mom says you can't play with anything that shoots bullets? Ok, then... You can take the water gun. It doesn't have bullets, but it's really dangerous. It shoots this snake spit that burns your enemies. You shoot them in the eye and their face becomes all red and explodes! You know, I think I'll keep the water gun. The black pirate is the only one who knows how to shoot snake spit.

You can have... The deadly sword of the Caribbean! What? You can't play with swords? Well... Ok, here. You can take my sister's magic wand. If the white pirate touches his enemy with this evil wand, a gooey spider web gets them and they can't breathe and become all blue. Wait, I think the black pirate should have the wand, because he's evil.

The white pirate? What can he have?

(Jack looks around, there's nothing left for his friend to play with.)

Well, he's really brave. He'll be OK.

Boy Monologue - Comedic

Children's Day

Ethan has got it all figured out. He's proclaimed a new holiday for kids to do what they like.

ETHAN:

OK, Mom and Dad. I thought about this really hard and I decided our family should have a new holiday called *Children's Day*. Mom, you have Mother's Day and Dad has Father's Day. I think it's only fair I have a day too.

This is a day where I would be *appreciated*. In the morning, you and Dad would praise me for not cleaning my room and not eating my vegetables, then make me a chocolate and bubble gum omelet for breakfast... with gummy bears on the side.

After breakfast, we would walk around the house looking for things to break and ways to annoy my little sister (this is Children's Day, by the way, not baby day). Then we'd go to Disneyland *and* Legoland. When we get home, we'll jump on all the beds until we feel sick, crayon on the walls and stick Play-Doh on all the furniture. After dinner, you would all have to go to bed while I stayed up playing all night with my friends making a big mess.

How do you like my idea? Wait! Before you say no, think about the bright side. It would only be once a year!

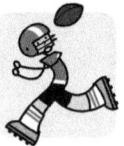

Boy Monologue - Dramatic

Why Did You Change Me

Ever since he got glasses and braces, Buddy has been picked on at school. In this monologue, he complains to his mom about his changed image.

BUDDY:

They don't want to play with me, all right? None of the other kids want to play with me. I tried to do what you said. I really tried. I went up to Cole, the coolest kid in the class, and asked him if he wanted to share our lunches. He was smiling so I thought everything was going really well, and then he took my peanut butter and jelly sandwich out of my lunchbox and he left with his friends.

He took my sandwich and just said, "Thank you, *Butt.*"

That's what they call me, *Butt.*

It's all your fault, mom. Everything was fine until you took me to that eye doctor and made me wear the bug glasses. It made me lose my friends. But nobody called me Butt then. Then you took me to the dentist and made me wear these ugly, disgusting rail tracks in my mouth! Don't you care, mom? Why did you change me from Buddy to Butt? Why didn't you love me the way I was?

Boy Monologue - Dramatic

Why Can't You Stop Fighting

Devon has been listening to his parents fight for months. Here, he decides to take a stand to protect himself and his little sister.

DEVON:

Why can't you stop it! Why can't you stop yelling at each other? You think we don't hear you up there? You think kids only hear when you speak really nice and slow? You think when you close the door to our bedroom at night we just turn off like that stupid talking doll you got Bella?

Well guess what, Mom and Dad, we can hear everything! Including the part when you say, "If I didn't have kids, I would leave you", Mom. And Dad when you say, "be my guest, you don't care about the kids anyway".

So we want to tell you, "Go for it". Get a divorce. We've been listening to you fighting all this time but you're always saying the same thing. Dad, you're broke. Mom, you spend too much money. Mom, you complain too much. And Dad, you drink too much. Dad, you wanted kids, and Mom, you didn't. That's it, right? I didn't forget anything? So get it over with already and let us sleep!

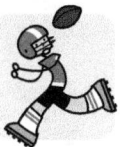

Boy Monologue - Dramatic

The Baseball Game

Hudson tells his dad how he hit a home run in his Little League baseball game only to find out his dad didn't share the moment with him.

HUDSON:

I know it's not your fault Dad. I know you really wanted to be at my baseball game. I know when you promised you'd be there you didn't know you would have to stay at work. I know you didn't have a choice... and you love me.

But Dad, I played so well. I hit a home run. I didn't even feel like playing when I saw your seat empty, but Mom said she had you on the phone and would give you a play by play of everything I did. So I thought maybe if I'm really good you would just forget about your job and come see for yourself.

And that's when I hit the home run. It felt so good! Everybody was cheering. Mom was jumping up and down. I looked for the phone in her hand but she had left it on the empty chair. And then I knew she lied. She wasn't talking to you at all. She was just pretending so I wouldn't be sad. So I walked out. I just ran away.

(beat)

I didn't want to be there. Just like you.

MONOLOGUES FOR KIDS
AGES 11-13 YEARS OLD

Girl Monologue - Comedic

My life is a Circus

Angelina talks about her unusual circus life and how she copes with her parents' extravagance.

ANGELINA:

My parents are clowns. No, literally, my parents *are* clowns. I am the offspring of two clowns who juggle, pirouette, and throw buckets of paint at each other all day. Really, I am not joking. No one ever believes me when I say I live in a circus. Ok, so I'm not part of the act – yet – but my life is a circus. No set meal times, or bed time, or checking on my homework. Everything is always "up in the air"... and swinging on a trapeze.

But now I'm taking matters into my own hands:

"Mom, I'm going to count to 3, if you're not here in 3 seconds, you're not getting ice cream tonight."

"Dad, come tell me to clean my room!"

To be fair, they have tried to do the parent thing for a while, but it's hard to be taken seriously when you have a big red nose and giant grin on your face. All my friends complain their parents won't let them be who they really are, so I just make sure my parents don't feel they have to change. They're happy and they love me. What else could a kid want?

Girl Monologue - Comedic

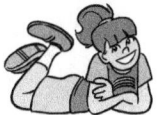

How to Skip School

Julia teaches a friend how to skip school and not get caught.

JULIA:

If you want to skip school, do what I do, think like a criminal: make sure there are no witnesses, cover your tracks, have an alibi and destroy incriminating evidence.

No witnesses means no brother or sister who can tell your parents you weren't at school.

To cover your tracks, prepare for school like any other day. Dress for school, take all your schoolwork with you and leave on time.

My alibi is my best friend Carrie. She meets me at the 7-11 after school to fill me in on anything that happened in class so I sound totally realistic when Mom asks, "How was your day?"

Before everyone gets home, I erase the incriminating evidence. I press the delete button on the answering machine and there goes the message from the principal about my absence.

Voila! All I have left to do is forge a note from my parents about how I suffered a bad case of food poisoning. By the way, food poisoning is the best excuse for being absent one day. You bounce back in 24 hours and there's a no questions asked guarantee. After all, no one wants to hear about your puke!

Girl Monologue - Comedic

Graduation Speech Payback

Abigail is graduating from Junior High. She decides to take this opportunity to tell everyone about how everything will change in High School and how the nerds will rule.

ABIGAIL:

Well, we've made it through Junior High and I'm sure everybody's very excited about getting to High School. But I don't think anybody is as excited as I am. And since I'm valedictorian and I get to make the speech, I'll tell you why.

Up till now, the winners in school have been the ones who are cute and have their cliques. The losers have been the loners with the glasses and braces. Up till now, the winners have been the cool kids who don't study and the losers have been the nerdy types who win the science fair.

Well, that's all going change in High School.

The cute girls will get zits and buckteeth. The nerdy girls will have perfect teeth and contact lenses. New school, new rules. Everyone will have to make friends all over again and it will come down to survival of the fittest. The Junior High School loners will adapt quickly while the cliquey girls will still be wondering why sticking gum in someone's hair doesn't make you popular anymore.

And finally, the cool girls who didn't study will know nothing. They'll hide behind cheerleading for a while, but end up single moms counting the years to the high school reunion, while the nerdy girls will rule the world. The countdown is on. See you in High School!

Girl Monologue - Dramatic

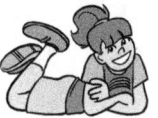

The Places We'll Go

Laura tells her English teacher how much she will miss him next school year.

LAURA:

Hi, Mr. Sanders. Can I come in? I left some of my books behind... on purpose. I just wanted to say goodbye.

I don't want the year to be over. I know I should be excited but after the summer break, I'll be in a new class and have Mrs. Parks for English. Everyone says she's boring and just follows the book. You never follow the book. I don't want to be in her class. I don't think she even likes literature. She does tons of vocabulary and gives a test every week.

You know I'm not a very good test taker. But I got much better in your class.

Do you know what my favorite day was this year? It was the day we were taking our big second semester English exam. I was so stressed out I bit all my nails. Then you came in with a book by Dr. Seuss and said that to celebrate "Reading Across America Week", we would start with a favorite story of yours, "Oh, the Places You'll Go". You had us gather around you, sitting on the floor like little kids all over again. And all of a sudden I felt like I could do the test, like it would be easy, because you cared, and you believed in us.

Mr. Sanders, I wish you could see the places we'll go.

Girl Monologue - Dramatic

The Diet

Kaneisha is starving herself to lose weight. In this monologue, she stands up to her mom who wants her to eat.

KANEISHA:

I'm not hungry, I said! I'm just not hungry and you can't make me eat! I'm not a kid anymore and I get to decide what goes into my body. Maybe if you didn't stuff me like a turkey with your cupcakes and pies when I was growing up I wouldn't be so fat now!

I said *fat*, and I'm tired of you lying to me about the way I really look. I'm fat, so say it like it is. That's what everyone at school calls me. They laugh at the pants you make me squeeze into. I can't breathe in any of my clothes because you won't admit your daughter is... obese!

So the least you can do is let me try to lose weight instead of acting hurt when I turn down your cooking. I had a boiled egg and a half grapefruit for lunch and that's enough. Maybe if I stop eating completely I'll get one day of peace at school, even maybe one friend.

Don't you see, mom? They're all laughing at me. I'm a blob. I feel blown up and empty inside, just like one of your donuts.

Girl Monologue - Dramatic

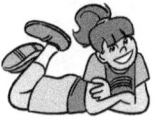

Shoplifting

Sophia, a young girl from a rough neighborhood, has been caught shoplifting shoes. In this monologue, she tries to convince the shop owner to let her go.

SOPHIA:

I wasn't shoplifting! I just forgot to take the stupid shoes off, OK? Here, take them back. I don't want them anyway. They're ugly. The red glitters are coming off already and the heels are too low.

Give me my old sneakers back. Can I go now?

(beat)

Oh, come on. I'm not even thirteen yet. What are you going to do, arrest me? You're going to call my dad, really? (laughs) Well, good luck with that! Maybe when the police come, they can help you look for him in *jail*.

(beat)

No, don't call social services, please. I'm sorry. I'll tell the truth. I wanted the shoes so bad, I thought if I just walk out with them no one will notice. I didn't mean to get in trouble. I'll do whatever you say. I won't do it again. I promise. Please don't have these people take me away. You didn't want me to take your shoes away. Well, it's the same thing. So don't take me away. Please, don't steal me from my mom.

Boy Monologue - Comedic

She Loves Me... Not

Richard has just gotten a few signs from a girl he likes at school that she may like him too. Or maybe he just interpreting the signs wrong.

RICHARD:

Yes! She likes me! She likes me! Wow! This is the coolest thing on earth. She's in love. She said so... Well, almost. I mean, it was pretty clear to me.

First, she smiled. And she never smiles. Well, not since she got the braces. I like her braces, I think they look cool, but you know how girls are. But this time she just had to smile, because... well, that's the effect I have on girls, I guess.

Anyway, she smiled, which is a really good sign. And then, she even talked to me. She said, "Can I borrow your pen". Now, this can seem normal when you need a pen, but then she wrote a phone number, which looks to me like an excuse. If she just needed someone's phone number, why not put it straight into her cellphone? Well, we're not supposed to pull out cellphones in class, but still... I think she wanted me, not the pen.

And here's the proof. She said, "Bye, Rich" at the end of class. Now, nobody calls me that except my mom! So that shows she was getting really personal. They all say Richard at school because there's two of us. Oh, but wait a minute. There *is* two of us! And the other Rich was sitting right next me. Oh, NO!!! She was writing *his* number down. What a fool! Hey, give me that pen back!

Boy Monologue - Comedic

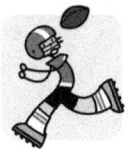

Vote Adam for Class President

Adam has decided to run for class president. Here, he makes an unusual speech to his classmates to try to rally the troops.

ADAM:

Citizens of 6th grade, I have heard you. It took me a while to decide to run for office, because I wanted to make sure I was worthy of such fine classmates, but now I know we're all in this together.

As most of you know, I hold the record for most detentions. I think that makes me the perfect candidate. After all, we live in a dictatorship. Mrs. Buggles, our English teacher, and Mr. Hornshoe, the Math teacher, have taken away our first amendment right to free speech. As the one student with nothing to lose, it's my duty to stand up for my oppressed classmates.

If you vote for me, there's a lot I will do for you as class president. I will demand bigger lockers, longer recess and the right to listen to music in class. I will go further than any class president has ever been. Citizens of 6th grade... I have a dream. I dream of a day with no homework, no grades, no teachers... no school at all!

But until that day, vote for me. Go Adam! Adam for class president!

(Note: 6th grade can be changed to 7th or 8th grade to fit your child's age.)

Boy Monologue - Comedic

Take Me to the Movies

Victor is using every trick in the book to convince his older brother to take him along to the movies with his friends.

VICTOR:

Please take me with you to the movies. Mom said I could go if I stayed with you. Please! I promise I won't embarrass you in front of your friends. I won't talk about the time you didn't want to go to school because you had a big zit on your nose or the time you watched a Miley Cyrus movie with Mom. Naturally, I won't say anything to Lindsay about how that other girl stayed all afternoon at our place last weekend or about the fact you pay me to tune your guitar because you really can't play.

(Victor gets an evil younger brother look on his face.)

Of course, I won't say anything, even if you don't take me with you. But you know... I may just forget *not to tell everyone*. Now don't get mad... Stop! You can't hit me. I'm four years younger than you. Lindsay would call you a coward and Mom would ground you anyway. I'm sure we can come to an agreement...

You'll take me? Really? Thank you! That's really nice of you. And I didn't even have to ask...

(beat)

Oh, by the way, I'll also need 5 bucks for popcorn.

Boy Monologue - Dramatic

Foreclosure

Andrew and his mom have just come home to find an eviction notice on the front door.

ANDREW:

Don't cry, Mom. It's just a piece of paper. It's just a stupid orange tag. It doesn't mean anything. It says "eviction notice", so it's just a notice, it doesn't mean we have to go now. They can't make us leave if we have nowhere to go.

(beat)

They can't make us leave anyway! Not if we don't want to. I'll fight them, mom. I'll stand right here and block the door and tell them it's our home! They can come in over my dead body if they want.

(Andrew snatches the tag from the door and crumples it.)

Here, I took off the tag, Mom. It's gone. Don't cry. We'll be OK. You always said as long as we're together we're OK, right? I don't need a house. I don't even need my bedroom. We can sell my things and rent a small studio. I always wanted my bed to be a pullout couch in front of the TV. I bet all my friends would think it's the coolest thing. We could watch movies all night and have a great time.

Come on, smile. Who needs a house when you can share a room with a cool kid like me?

Boy Monologue - Dramatic

The Class Bully

Billy has been bullying others at school, but now he's starting to realize he doesn't like what he's become and tries to change his image.

BILLY:

Hey, kid! Hey, wait, I'm not gonna punch you! Hey, come over here. I am gonna punch you if you don't bring your butt over here right now!

Why are you going around telling people I'm a bully? Did I ever hit you? I did? Well, maybe you deserved it, did you ever think about that? Come on, let's go over there where no one can hear us, I want to tell you something. You don't have to be scared, I promise.

Listen... You know you're a nerd, right? Well, were you always a nerd or did people start calling you nerd and you kind of didn't have a choice? It's the same for me, see. It started with Cindy. She didn't want to be my girlfriend so I pulled her hair in class. That made some kids laugh, so I kept going. With other girls. And then with nerds like you.

Now I can pick anybody in the playground and make them hate going to school overnight. They all laugh cause they're all scared of me. They never tell. You're the first kid to do that. So I'm not sure if I should kick your butt or respect you.

Hey, listen. I'm sick of being the bully. Maybe we can help each other. What do you say?

Boy Monologue - Dramatic

Goodbye to Grandpa

Alex is visiting his dying grandpa in the hospital for the last time but doesn't know how to say goodbye.

ALEX:

Hey Grandpa, how are you doing today?

I'm sorry, that's the wrong question to ask. I just wanted to make you feel better.

Do these tubes hurt in your nose? No? That's good.

I'm sorry. I don't know what to say, Grandpa. I like it better when you can talk.

Remember when I came to visit you last year and you got these front row tickets for the Red Sox game? You said you didn't like anything more than baseball. That's one of the best days of my life, Grandpa. I'm sorry I didn't play baseball sooner... But I'm in the League now. Did you hear that, Grandpa?

Mom and Dad say it's better if I don't come anymore... Well, you know, I have to get back to school. So I have to say goodbye now. But I don't know how to.

I brought you my favorite baseball card. I figured if you don't like anything more than baseball, you would know what that means to me. Grandpa, I don't know if you can hear me, but... I don't want to ever get it back. Promise?

About the Author

Alex Swenson has worked as an actor, writer and film editor for the past 15 years in New York and Los Angeles. She created the website www.Acting-School-Stop.com to help new and aspiring actors get the information they need to succeed. The website offers free step by step information on how to become an actor, a guide to acting schools, acting biz tutorials, online acting classes and a wide range of acting resources for actors of all levels.

Alex Swenson also publishes a newsletter, *The Acting School Monthly*, with monthly acting tips, as well as a blog. You can visit the Acting School Stop website to subscribe to each. You can also find Alex Swenson on Facebook, YouTube and Twitter.

Facebook: www.facebook.com/ActingSchoolStop

Twitter: www.twitter.com/ActingStop

YouTube: www.youtube.com/ActingSchoolStop

"My 11-yr daughter is acting. Last fall, we signed with an LA agent and manager. The business is still quite new to me. I just started reading your website. It's EXTREMELY helpful! Looking forward to reading it all! Thanks so much." Cindy Nishijima (Mother to Shari, 13 years old) San Francisco Bay Area

"I just wanted to tell you that I think this is an AMAZING newsletter. It contains so much valuable information that basically guides the new actor and teaches the veterans how to stay focused. Being new to auditions, reels, headshots, "what to do", "what not to do" etc... it has literally made my life so much easier. I can't thank you enough for all the guidance and positive reinforcement. It's priceless. Thank you." Akira Binns, actress